Summer Camp to Survival Show Winner:
A Scout's Story

Terry L. Fossum

Special thanks to my partner on the show, Natalie Casanova, whose strength, wisdom, and intestinal fortitude made winning possible. There's no way in the world I could have done it without her!

Summer Camp to Survival Show Winner: A Scout's Story

ISBN: 978-0-9885854-7-8

Printed in the United States of America, First edition

The goal of every Scout is to become an Honorable Man or Woman.

– Terry Fossum

Dedication

This book is dedicated to all the Scouting professionals and volunteers who sacrifice so much of their time and energy to influence the lives of youth around the world. Sometimes it may not feel as if you're making a difference. I can tell you, without question, that you are.

It's also dedicated to all the kids in the program. You are the true leaders of the movement. You are the reason it exists. You're creating a legacy that will be passed down for generations, and it's a legacy you can be proud of.

Keep up the energy. Keep up the vision. Keep up the Good Fight.

You give me hope.

Terry

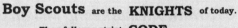

Other books by Terry L. Fossum:

Secrets of a Network Marketing Millionaire

Passion To Move Mountains – The Oxcart Technique

The S.I.M.P.L.E. Guide to Public Speaking –
  Without Losing Your Lunch

Regarding these books, as well as other audio series,
  you can find Terry at his website:

www.TerryLFossum.com

and on Facebook:

www.facebook.com/TerryLFossum/

Table of Contents

In Scouting,
the Journey
IS
the Destination

- Terry L. Fossum
Scoutmaster, Troop 400

Introduction

Imagine this: One morning you get an email from a major television network, saying they're interested in putting you on a brand-new reality TV show that pits 10 survival experts against each other in a jungle somewhere in the world, and your partner will be a complete novice – someone who has never even been in the outdoors before, someone who thinks roughing it means staying in a four-star hotel without room service.

What would you think?

First of all, probably that it was a hoax, right?

Yeah, me, too.

In fact, I kind of hoped that it was.

But what if you checked into it and found it was real?

Oh, crud!

Could you do it?

Would you do it?

Okay, let's add to that. Let's say you're old. I mean like, *really* old. Like 52 years old. And you knew you would be the oldest person on the show. You'd be competing against strong young men and women in their 20s and 30s.

How about now?

Let's add more:

And what if you knew you were going up against real hardcore survivalists? Like military survival instructors, Special Forces guys, record-setting distance-hikers and those sorts, and your only background is that you were a Boy Scout?

Would you do it then?

And what if you knew that the novice they were teaming you up with would be the complete opposite of you?

What would that person be like? What would they look like?

Could you stand being with them for up to an entire month, 24 hours a day, trying to get them to do what they need to do to survive in an environment that is as foreign to them as Mars?

And what would it be like to try to do this while starving to death, completely sleep deprived, exhausted, covered in bugs, sleeping in a shelter with no blankets or anything, in the rain, not showering at all for an entire month, while competing in survival skills competitions with people who do this sort of thing for a living?

How about now?

Let's add one more detail: You're going to be in your Scout uniform the entire time, so therefore representing all of Scouting, while being filmed every single minute of every day. Even while you're sleeping, trying to have a private conversation, and everything else. And the entire Scouting community – heck, millions of people around the world – will be judging every single thing you say and do, because you're representing Scouting. While sleep deprived, starving, and all of that. No pressure at all...

Crazy, right?

Well, that's what happened to me, and that's just what I did.

My competitors, including a warlord, a ninja, two U.S. Air Force survival instructors, U.S. Special Forces guys, and more.

My qualifications: I'm a Boy Scout.

I mean, we think our Scouting skills are good. We hope they are. But are they *really*?

Without question.

I won.

Can you believe it? A brand-new survival reality TV show on an actual network, Season 1, pitted against nine of the toughest people you'll ever meet, and the Boy Scout won!

My name is Terry L. Fossum, and I'm an Eagle Scout. And, I'm also a Scoutmaster.

Wait a minute – you mean one of those guys with his belly hanging over his belt, sitting in a lawn chair with a cup of coffee constantly in his hand? Yep. That's me.

And this is my story.

Now, I understand that this is just one of millions of Scouting stories around the world, but it's the one I know best, because it's mine.

If it weren't for Scouting, I would probably be on drugs, or in a gang, or dead.

See, Scouting changed my life. In fact, Scouting probably saved my life.

Here's how:

Chapter 1

On the Wrong End of an Assault Rifle

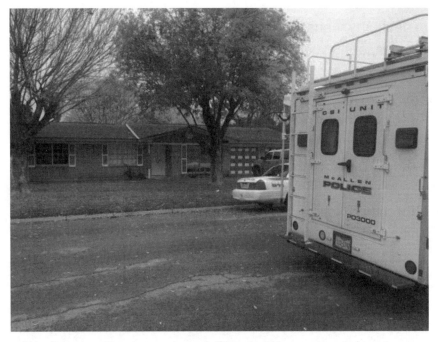

Front page of our newspaper! The drug house next door to my home has an armed standoff between the dealers that live there and the drug cartel.

To understand the impact Scouting has had on my life, it's important to know where I started.

I'm proud to say I grew up in McAllen, Texas, a small U.S./Mexico border town in the Rio Grande Valley of Texas. I really love McAllen. Some of the best people you will ever meet live there, the weather is fantastic year 'round, and the food is off the charts. I truly miss many things about

McAllen. But it could be a little rough growing up there. Kids who come from the Rio Grande Valley have a special form of toughness. A toughness that sticks with them for the rest of their lives.

In fact, my house was recently on the front page of the newspaper! Well, you couldn't actually see my house because the Crime Scene Investigation (CSI) truck was in the way. Apparently a couple of armed gunmen busted into the drug house next door because the drug dealers there owed them money, and you do *not* want to owe those guys money.

My brother actually got shot at while on a troop campout. They were camped right on the Rio Grande River and he was sitting on the bank hanging out. Suddenly there was a puff of smoke in the dirt beside him, followed by a clapping noise from the other side of the river. *That's weird,* he thought. Then it happened again. *What the heck is that?* he wondered. When it happened a third time, he realized, *Crap! Someone is shooting at me from Mexico!* Time to go.

On one of my campouts, I was sleeping in my tent and heard a truck coming into camp. *That's right,* I thought. *Mr. Whiteside was going to be coming in late.* About five minutes later, the camp filled with headlights from trucks rushing into camp, one after another after another. *What the heck?!* I wondered. Apparently Mr. Whiteside had tripped a Border Patrol sensor while driving out to us, and they thought we were a group of illegal aliens.

Ah, the joys of camping on the border.

When I was about 14 years old, I was in my back yard one night, and I heard a noise in my back alley. Understand, when you're from my neighborhood and you hear a noise, you check it out. So I jumped over our fence into the dark alley. That's not the best situation. You don't really want to be in my alley at night.

Then it got bad.

Suddenly headlights hit me. There was a car back there. Now, a car probably means an adult, and an adult in my back alley at that time of night usually means a drug deal, or a robbery, or worse – none of which they want a 14-year-old boy to witness. And there I was, completely exposed with lights shining directly on me.

Then it got worse.

Suddenly a guy walked out in front of those headlights with an assault rifle and aimed it right at me.

I didn't dare run. If you run, that makes you prey and the man with the gun becomes a predator. Not to mention, I can't run faster than a bullet. So I stood my ground as he walked up to me. After a few minutes of talking with me, he either decided I wasn't worth the trouble, or he was feeling charitable, and let me walk away.

That was when I was in middle school. When I was in high school, my father was killed.

Before he died, one of the neighbors came up to him and said, "I just want to make sure you understand something: Not a single one of your boys will ever grow up to be anything."

Think about it: He was talking about me and my brothers. That was the expectation. Probably that we would be in a gang, like so many others. Or on drugs. Or dealing. Or dead.

But there was something he didn't know: We were in Boy Scouts.

See, we were a Scouting family. Before he was killed, my dad was the Committee Chair for our troop. Mom was a Den Leader. They understood that Scouting taught morals and values that we might not learn on the street. It taught us that right was right, even if no one else was doing it, and wrong was wrong, even if everyone else was doing it. It taught us skills we would use for the rest of our lives. It taught us to Be Prepared. For Life.

Both of my older brothers were Scouts. I started off as a "den mascot" before I was old enough to even join Cub Scouts. I'm glad they have Lion Scouts now, so 5-year-olds can join.

I took to it right away. I just thought it was fun. We did cool stuff. We had adventures.

What I didn't realize was that, little by little, Scouting was shaping my life. It was forming who I was. It was going to teach me what I needed to know not only to succeed in life, but also to make a difference in the world. To become a successful businessman, and military officer, and author, and public speaker, and to fund philanthropic causes around the world. Never in a million years would I have thought that I'd use those skills to win a survival reality TV show!

Chapter 2

Being a Scout

Terry taking a break while backpacking.

Finally! I was 7 years old. I could become a Cub Scout! We got to do all sorts of cool stuff at den meetings and pack meetings (read: run around like maniacs). My dad and I built pinewood derby cars together (okay, he did most of it), Blue and Gold Banquets had awesome cakes for dessert (I think other stuff happened, but I mostly remember the desserts), and we learned knots and first aid and other big-boy stuff. The best part: I looked seriously cool in my uniform! (I thought I did, anyway.) Both my mom and my dad were there with me, and that was important. Scouts are more successful if at least one of their parents is involved, and it was really good family time, too. My mom wasn't just my mom – she was a Den Leader! That meant she was in charge! And Dad was a Committee Member, so he was working behind the scenes, leading by example.

And then I crossed over into Webelos, and it just kept on getting better. We started doing more outdoor stuff. We got to actually go camping. That's where the real adventure is.

I'll never forget putting on the "Denner" cords in Webelos. The Denner was the boy leader of the Webelos Den. For the first time, I was being called a leader. I wasn't expected merely to follow – I was expected to lead. No one had told me I was a leader before. But somebody believed enough in me to give me those cords, and it was a turning point in my life.

As Denner, I helped set up before the meeting and keep control during it. (As if that's possible at a Webelos meeting.) It started giving me some responsibility. It taught me to be not part of the problem, but part of the solution. It taught me to give back, not just show up and expect everyone else to do everything. It taught me to serve.

I loved Cub Scouts and Webelos, but the real adventure starts with Boy Scouts.

Right away, you're put into a patrol of about 6–8 boys. Get this: My first patrol leader's dad owned a candy company.

Our patrol meetings were in the warehouse! All the candy we could eat!

I didn't miss a single patrol meeting. (But was usually pretty wired by the time I got home.)

I didn't miss a single campout, either, and that's where the real fun, and the real learning, happens. It's crazy how much you learn as a new Scout. You go from being afraid of the dark to becoming a master of the wilderness! You're roaming around the woods where many people wouldn't dream of going, and you live there in a tent, or less.

Before long, I became the Patrol Leader of the mighty Cobra Patrol. It was awesome! We had patrol meetings every single week: During the first half we worked on Scout skills, and in the second half we played hide-and-go-seek around my neighborhood. I know: maybe not the smartest idea, in my neighborhood. We mixed in fun with the learning, and it worked for us.

But I started to hone my skills at leadership. I did some things well. I did some things really poorly. And Scouting was a safe place for me to mess up, and keep learning.

And then things changed.

It's important to find a troop that's a good fit for you. Every troop has a different feel to it; every troop has a different culture. And sometimes that culture changes. Sometimes you need to change troops. But whatever you do, stay in Scouting.

Our Scoutmaster, Bob Helbing, one of the greatest people on the face of the earth as far as I'm concerned, quit. A new guy came on who meant well, but wasn't really engaged. The culture of the troop changed.

Bullying became the norm. Cussing, playing mean tricks on other Scouts, all sorts of bad stuff. It wasn't Scouting any more. It wasn't fun. Especially when you're one of the boys being picked on.

It was time to quit.

Chapter 3

Summer Camp

Terry's first year on Summer Camp Staff.

Summer camp was the coolest place on earth for me.

That's where I got to see real Scouting happening. It was like utopia: Everything was perfect there. People were having fun. Kids my age would act like idiots – singing, doing goofy skits, telling dumb jokes; it was awesome!

What makes summer camp great is the people, the enthusiasm, and the culture. Youth teaching other youth by their own example what it's like to be a good person, what it's like to be a leader.

We went to the same camp every year: Camp Perry in the Rio Grande Valley. Camp Perry epitomized the Scout Oath and Law.

As far as camps go, it was far from fancy. It didn't have the newest facilities. It didn't have a zip line, or a climbing wall, or anything like that. But it had the most important thing of all: It had Scouting. REAL Scouting.

The staff was full of the best people I had ever even imagined. They had so much enthusiasm! They taught that in Scouting you didn't pick on people, you were nice to them. They taught that it really was cool to be trustworthy, and loyal, and all of that stuff.

This was the Scouting I wanted.

I thought to myself, *Man, it would be great to be one of those camp staff members, but I doubt I'm good enough. These people get up in front of everyone and lead songs and stuff.* They were heroes to me. I was just the skinny 13-year-old kid who got picked on a lot.

My mom encouraged me.

"Well, if you want to be part of that, why don't you apply?"

"Because I doubt I'm good enough! I don't know how to lead songs, and teach merit badges, and be totally awesome like that."

"They didn't either when they started. They learned, just like you will. They'll help you. You should at least try."

I'll never forget going in for that interview. I had never been in an interview before. I was scared. I still have the application I gave the Camp Director. I'm not sure I looked him in the eyes once during the whole thing. But as happens with so many Scouters (adult Scouts), he saw something in me that I didn't see in myself. He believed in me. And that helped me believe in myself.

Another step toward becoming who I am today.

When I was chosen to be on staff, I made a whopping $6 a week; but it wasn't about the pay. It was about being part of something awesome. And get this: I became the Nature Director. Do you *think* that might have had an effect on who I've become?

There I was among my idols: Jason Hughes and Jim Taylor. Chris Boswell and Charlie Ward. These guys were legends among Scouts in the Rio Grande Valley. I couldn't believe I got to walk with the giants.

What I didn't realize was that Scouting was teaching me to become one of them. I found out that I was actually pretty good at getting up front and acting like an idiot!

Wait a minute…

Oh, well. Truth hurts…!

In year after year of being on staff, I gained confidence as I learned to teach merit badges and lead songs. I learned to whip up a camp full of boys into an excited frenzy.

Get this: I actually became… popular! Now, there's a feeling I knew nothing about. But kids would come running up to me whenever they would see me. And when they could pick a staff member to eat meals with them, I was usually one of the first chosen.

Talk about a confidence booster! In my troop, I was one of the kids getting picked on all the time. Here, people liked me. Maybe I *was* okay. Maybe I *was* worth liking. Maybe I was actually a leader.

I met a very small troop while on staff, Troop 63. I think they had about six boys, and they were all younger than me, but those boys were nice. They had great spirit. In fact, this young, tiny troop won the Spirit Award for their entire week at camp – the top award given.

When I asked them if I could join their troop, they couldn't believe I wanted to. What they didn't realize was that their kindness and true Scout spirit was exactly what I was looking for in Scouting.

Thank God I didn't quit Scouting. Instead, I found a troop that exemplified what I was looking for. That's why I recommend interviewing several troops when joining Boy Scouts; different troops have different ways of doing things, and you have to find the one that fits you best. And, whatever you do, don't quit Scouts.

As the Senior Patrol Leader, or boy in charge of my new troop, I gained leadership experience that I've drawn from throughout the rest of my life. My Scoutmaster, Jerry White, was my mentor, and he worked with me every step of the way.

When I was 19, during the summer of my freshman year of college, they asked me to be Program Director for the entire camp, even though you weren't legally able to do it without a waiver until you were 21. I jumped at the chance.

I know I'll say something was "life-changing" about a million times in this book; but it's true. Sometimes our lives change with one dramatic event, and sometimes they change with a series of smaller, but significant, ones. I think Scouting is all about the latter. It's designed so that each event builds on the ones before it.

A skyscraper isn't built starting with the top floor. It starts with a solid foundation. Then each floor is built on top of that, and so on.

That's the way Scouting does it, every step of the way.

Being on camp staff was a very important step in my growth.

By the way, remember that troop I quit? Their culture has changed again, and they're back to being awesome. Both my brothers' names hang on the wall as Eagle Scouts of Troop 7 – something we're all very proud of. They're listed on a board that my dad made when he was the Committee Chair, not long before he died.

Summer Camp was one of the biggest growth experiences of my life, and the next step would shape how I lived that life forever.

Chapter 4

Order of the Arrow

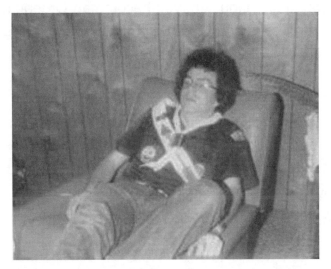

Terry exhausted after a full day in the OA.

The next huge step in my growth can be spelled with two letters: OA. The Order of the Arrow (OA) shaped my entire life – no exaggeration.

The OA is an honor organization within Scouting that recognizes Scouts and Scouters who best exemplify the Scout Oath and Law in their daily lives. It teaches service to others in a big way.

It may be the thing that kept me interested in Scouting as I got older. I had already done everything I could in the troop: I had been the Senior Patrol Leader (SPL), JASM, Instructor, pretty much everything. I needed a new challenge, and even though I stayed somewhat active in my troop, the OA provided that extra challenge that kept me excited.

When you're first inducted, you become an Ordeal member. You go through a couple of cool ceremonies, and spend a weekend doing service projects without talking. It truly teaches you to serve without complaining, and to "turn your thoughts inward" – basically, to stop yammering on all the time, and shut up and think for once. Being an Ordeal member was amazing. I'll never forget that incredible meal at the end of the weekend, and the night of learning Indian lore that followed. I can still hear the beat of the drums and the singing, and remember how great it felt to learn the ancient dance. Awesome.

But if I thought Ordeal was cool, it was *nothing* compared to the next level: brotherhood. I learned more in that one-hour ceremony than I probably learned in the rest of my life about taking a burden from others, and becoming part of a brotherhood that was dedicated to making the world a better place. It truly changed me forever. I strive hard each day of my life to complete the challenges given to me in that ceremony. Some days I succeed; some days I fail. But every day, I try.

I joined the ceremony team so I could be part of putting on those cool ceremonies. My buddies and I would practice in our back yards so we could memorize the lines and not read them during the ceremonies. We worked together and built our own costumes so we looked the parts. We had competitions in our lodge to see who had the best team, and the winners got to put on the ceremony for the new candidates. We loved seeing their freaked-out looks as they entered our fire bowl. Then they were even more freaked out when… Well, you'll have to go through your Brotherhood to see what I mean…

I was blown away at being chosen as a Vigil Honor member at the age of 17. Vigil is the top level possible in the OA, something that few people ever attain. I have kept the Vigil, and learned the lessons that go all the way down to your soul. To this day, it's one of the things I'm proudest of, and one that had the most profound impact on me.

I still go by myself into the wilderness, away from the sounds of civilization, to listen to my God and His nature. In fact, as I'm writing this, I'm on my third day alone in the mountains of North Idaho.

In the OA, I became a Chapter Chief of a district, then Lodge Chief of the council, and then Section Vice-Chief for most of Texas.

As Section Vice-Chief, I traveled around to all the different lodges in the different councils and began a cross-flow of ideas between them. That was an incredible lesson that has helped me in my business and military careers! Let's see: Get the teams within an organization talking to each other and sharing ideas so that not only is communication better between them, but they can also all grow and become better as a result. Yep: More corporate executives could benefit from learning what I learned from Scouting when I was 19.

The Section Conference, where all of the lodges in the section get together at a college, was the very first place I spoke in front of a group of several hundred people, and received cheers and applause from all of them. I decided I liked that.

It was another Scouting skill that influenced my life forever, as I now speak to companies around the globe. And I learned it from Scouts, starting with being a patrol leader, then an SPL, being on camp staff, and then in the OA.

Even though I didn't realize it, Scouting had taught me skills and lessons I would apply throughout the rest of my life, and make history doing it.

Chapter 5

Corps of Cadets, Texas A&M University

Terry in his Corps of Cadets uniform. Notice the
Eagle Badge proudly worn on the uniform!

The Corps of Cadets at Texas A&M University is wild. It's
basically like ROTC, but more intense. MUCH more intense.
More cadets from A&M than from any other place, including
the military academies, end up becoming generals. That's
how tough the Corps is.

We had our own section on the campus, called the Quad. We had our own dining hall. We would wear World War II–style uniforms every day, to class and everywhere else. We would wake up way early for uniform inspection and all of the fun that went with it (read "fun"=lots of push-ups), have a full military formation, march to chow (breakfast), and rush back to our "rooms" to get ready for class that day.

Understand that Texas A&M is a world-class civilian university, so we did all of this in addition to tending to our normal class loads, in my case as a mechanical engineering student.

The Fish Drill Team (FDT) at A&M is a precision rifle drill team composed entirely of freshman in the Corps of Cadets. (Freshmen are known as "fish" in the Corps.) They do things with rifles that you didn't know could be done: spin them, throw them to each other, march in perfect precision – all at the same time. I decided it would be awesome to actually be one of them, so I went to the first practice.

"The Fish Drill Team will be the hardest thing you've ever done!" the Drill Sargent yelled. "You won't have time to eat, you won't have time to sleep, and if you think you're going to have time to have a girlfriend, you've got another think coming!"

That was my last practice.

The Corps Color Guard was also very cool. These are the guys who carry the flags for each of the services whenever the corps is on parade. I heard there were tryouts, so I thought I would check it out. The freshman positions were the guys to the left and the right of the flags who were holding the rifles. Extremely cool. What I didn't realize was that these positions always went to members of the Fish Drill Team, and as we just learned: That wasn't me.

Except.

Except that someone had made the decision that year that FDT members didn't have time to do this along with their normal practices, so the Color Guard positions would go to non-FDT members, starting this year.

So, I didn't get the job because I was great at drill. I didn't get the job because I was extraordinarily sharp. I got the job because I was the same height as another kid there, so we would look the same on either end.

Sometimes fate, or God (a Scout is reverent), has a way of making things happen.

Twice.

I was chosen by sheer luck (or Providence) to be on the head team that carried the Corps Colors in front of the entire Corps of Cadets. After being a rifle bearer my freshman year, I got to carry the actual Corps Flag my sophomore year – quite an honor. But when it came time to choose the leader for the entire Corps Color Guard the next year, the prior leader chose the other guy, my height-twin, to take over. I never asked why he didn't choose me; I just saluted smartly and carried on. (A Scout is obedient, even if he doesn't like it.)

There was a problem, though: The other guy wasn't a Scout. When it came time to show respect for the American flag, I guess no one ever showed him how. He wasn't trained like we Scouts were. After what happened one night, I'm surprised he's still alive.

At practice one evening, near the end of our sophomore year, he was screwing around with one of the other guys, and started chasing him around. With the American flag. Using it as a battering ram.

Bad idea.

Right at that point, one of the toughest seniors in the Corps of Cadets came walking by. Everyone knew this guy; he was scary. He was training to be Special Forces, and I'm sure he dreamed about killing people in his sleep. When he was in kindergarten.

Needless to say, the other guy was fired (I'm not sure if they ever found his body), and I was now in charge.

Okay, I thought, *now it's time. Now it's time to start putting that Boy Scout training to work.* I had learned to build up a patrol and a troop. Now it was time to take those skills out of the Scouting context and apply them elsewhere.

It was time to elevate the Corps Color Guard to a place it had never been before.

Step One: Unity. I learned this from being the OA Section Vice-Chief and visiting all the lodges: Pull the members together from the different service Color Guards (Army, Air Force, Navy) and get them to start seeing themselves as part of a bigger team, just like pulling patrols together as a troop, or OA lodges together as a section. We brainstormed ideas to make it better, and everyone got excited. We practiced together and got sharper than ever. I needed to give them a sense of identity, of unity. So, for the first time ever, we came up with Color Guard T-shirts. We were becoming a cohesive team.

Step Two: Logistics. We needed a place to meet, just as a troop does, so I worked with the Trigon (the military staff headquarters building) and secured a room on campus. Just as in camping, you need good gear, and you need to know how to take care of your gear. We made it happen.

Step Three: Above and beyond. Another place where we elevated our activities was at the football games. You know those HUGE flags that fly over college stadiums? The Color Guard would kind of shuffle out there and put up the flags before the games, no big deal.

But, what if we made it a big deal?

What if we marched in formation out there and did a real flag raising, just like we did in Scouts? Wouldn't that be cool?

29

It was.

It was awesome.

All the televised games would show us marching out there, and raising the flags to the National Anthem, sharp as could be.

Near the end of my junior year, I was completing my term as Cadet Sergeant in charge of the Color Guard. I felt good about it. The Color Guard had risen to a level I hoped it would – a level of professionalism that had not been seen before. I could leave that position knowing I had done my best, just as they'd taught me in Scouts. Just like a campsite, or anything else a Scout touches, I was leaving the Color Guard better than I had found it.

That wasn't good enough for the Corps.

"Cadet Fossum, you're not done yet," said Col. Buck Henderson, the military Color Guard Advisor.

"But I am, sir. I'm at the end of my junior year, and there is no position for a senior. I'm getting ready to choose my successor."

"Not so fast, cadet. You're not getting out of this so easily."

I was thoroughly confused, so he went on. "I can't tell you how impressed we are with what you've done here. In all the years of the Corps of Cadets, no one has ever elevated the Guard to this level, much less in this period of time. The staff here at the Trigon has discussed it, and we're making a change to the Corps. We want this level of professionalism to continue, so we're actually creating a senior, Command-level position: a Cadet Major in charge of the Corps Color Guard. And you're the first one ever."

I was floored.

All I had done was what I had learned in Scouting, and they changed history at Texas A&M because of it.

USA Today was doing an article on leadership and contacted the Trigon for people to interview. They sent them to me, among others. The paper wanted to know: Where had I learned this leadership? No question: Boy Scouts.

Chapter 6

Nuclear Warfare

Terry in cockpit of nuclear-equipped B-52.

As I mentioned before, my degree was in mechanical engineering (M.E.), so when I received a commission as an officer in the United States Air Force, I requested an engineering job in my home state: Texas.

Notice that I said "requested."

I learned that "requesting" is all you do with the military. You don't demand; you don't insist. At best, you recommend. But in truth, you request.

And that request was quickly thrown out the window, and I was instead given some non-engineering job in some place called Spokane, Washington (as in, "Where the heck is Spokane, Washington?!").

I was ticked! I'd worked hard for that M.E. degree. And I certainly didn't want to leave God's country: Texas!

My exact quote to the Colonel who gave me the assignment was: "That sucks, sir."

I know, I know: A Scout is obedient. Notice that I still called him "sir!" And, of course, I carried out my orders – very happily, as it turned out.

I learned that I was going to be spearheading a brand-new career field in the Air Force called "Operations Management," in the field's first graduating class.

I'd like to think I was selected because of my proven leadership skills, but in truth, it was probably because my engineering grades weren't all that good. Maybe it was both. Let's go with that.

So I went through the officer version of boot camp like a breeze. In fact, at one point near the end, the drill instructor finally came up to me and said, "I don't get it. I've done everything in the world to break you down, and there's nothing that bothers you!" Hey, once you've been a Senior Patrol Leader and gone through the Corps of Cadets, there's nothing in the world that can faze you!

I arrived at Fairchild Air Force base, assigned to the 325th Bombardment Squadron, an entire squadron of nuclear-equipped B-52s. Cool! We were one leg of our nation's nuclear triad, spending 24 hours a day on nuclear alert, as well as many other missions that I can't talk about here (or elsewhere, for that matter).

Keep in mind that one of the many things I liked about my hometown of McAllen is that it could be 80 degrees on Christmas day. My first winter in Spokane, it was minus 60 with the wind chill factor. Serious drag!

But believe it or not, I actually liked it. It felt like yet another Scouting adventure to me. *Okay, what obstacle do we get to overcome this time?*

And then I learned that "God's country" is actually everywhere – there's beauty everywhere. I fell in love with the mountains, and I learned that people can be great everywhere as well. The Pacific Northwest will forever be my home.

But when I arrived at the squadron, I learned something new: No one there had any idea what my job was. I was one of the first Adjutants in the Air Force since World War II, so no one had any idea! All they knew was that I worked directly for the Squadron Commander.

Hmmm, I thought to myself. *No one knows my job here. There has been no precedent. I guess I get to call the shots!*

It went something like this:

"What exactly IS your job here?"

(Realizing I can decide pretty much anything I want it to be): "Well, let me tell you…"

"Are you supposed to go through Prisoner of War training?"

(After seeing some of the other Second Lieutenants go through it and knowing that it would SUCK badly): "Um, NO, I'M NOT."

"Are you supposed to have flight gear?"

(Knowing that EVERYONE looks cool in a flight suit): "Um, YES, I AM."

"A form-fitted helmet and everything?"

(Pushing the envelope as far as I could go): "You betcha!"

Okay, so now I had all the cool gear. It was time to perform. And again, my Scout training allowed me to jump into action. I was the Commander's right-hand man for everything non-flying related. Okay, then I'd take it all. Scouts know how to work hard, and I worked my butt off.

Crews would land at 2 a.m., and I would still be working. I learned everything I could from anyone I could. I read manuals until I fell asleep; then I'd get up and do it all over again.

When the Inspector General came around, I was named one of the best in the Air Force. I started winning awards. I wasn't doing anything special; I was just doing what Scouts do: making sure everything was better than when I got there.

When they asked me to run my first squadron event, called a Dining In, I was all over it. Hey, Scouting had me up in front of people all the time; this was nothing new.

When those events were a success, they had me run events for the entire 92nd Bomb Wing. They had me emcee almost every event on base.

And then it happened.

Chapter 7

Executive Officer

Captain Terry Fossum in front of B-52 memorial
to his fallen friends.

Colonel Capitosti was the Director of Operations, now known as the Operations Group Commander. A group is basically a squadron of squadrons, and he was in charge of the war-fighting group on base, third in command of the entire Wing. But "Colonel C" was a screamer. He would fly off the handle more quickly than you can say "There goes my career."

But Colonel C liked me. And quite frankly, I liked him. I saw that he took good care of his people, if they were willing to work hard, and he knew I was willing to work hard.

He watched what I did at the squadron level and decided he wanted me to help him at the group level. So he did something that had never been done before: He asked me, a non-rated (non-flying) officer, to be his Executive Officer.

See, the Executive Officer position was always for the flyboys. Hey, this was a flying operation, so it only made sense. And it was a position for only the top up-and-coming aviator, the one who was expected to quickly go up the ranks.

And there I was, the first-ever non-rated Executive Officer for the 92d Operations Group.

Again, I found myself in a first-ever position, and again I knew I had Scouting to thank for it.

As before, I worked hard, and became the Officer of the Year for Fairchild Air Force Base.

On my dress blue uniform, I proudly wore my Eagle Scout ribbon – the only non-military ribbon allowed. The military understands the importance of Scouting and of being an Eagle Scout.

During all of that, even though I didn't have any kids of my own, I stayed involved in Scouting in any way I could. I helped start a new troop on base, ran camporees, acting as District Program Chair and as District Vice-Chair. I was the OA Advisor and worked with the ceremony teams.

I also got involved with other nonprofits in the area, so much so that the local community named me the United Way Volunteer of the Year (which put me on television several times a day), and I was even named the Humanitarian of the Year for all of Strategic Air Command.

The Pentagon called me up one day to discuss a potential new assignment with me.

"Go ahead," I said. "What have you got?"

"No, sir," the voice on the other end of the phone said, "I'm afraid we can't talk about it on the phone."

"Okay," I replied, "go ahead and call me on the STU-3." (That's the classified phone, the red phone like the one you've seen in the movies, where we could talk about nuclear war plans.)

"No, sir, I'm afraid that won't do."

"Why the heck not?"

"It's above that level, sir."

WHAT??? Above the level of the STU-3??? What the heck could that be???

"All I can tell you, sir… is that it's REALLY COOL. We'd like you to fly to the Pentagon so we can brief you on it."

I had other offers as well. I was being offered any job I wanted in the Air Force, in any career field, up to a Lieutenant Colonel rank; and I was a Junior Captain.

All of this is unheard of. And all of it is absolutely true. And all of it is because of Boy Scouts.

But I had decided that I was going to resign my commission, because I had started a direct sales business on the side, and things were going pretty well; so I never went to the Pentagon to find out what the assignment was. I'll always wonder….

At about the same time, I was chosen to attend Squadron Officer's School – again, quite an honor.

Again I put the skills I learned in Scouting to work, and became a Distinguished Graduate of the school.

And three days before I graduated, a gunman went through our base hospital, killing and maiming people along the way. And on the day I graduated, one of our hotshot pilots drove a B-52 into the ground, killing everyone on board, all of whom were friends of mine.

My final real job in the military was helping with the shooting victims and their families, trying to console them and get them the help they needed. It wasn't a fun job at all, but I volunteered for it. Scouting taught me that my duty was "to help other people at all times."

There was no glitz and no glamour. No big office, and no upward promotion. But it's one of the more rewarding things I've ever done, and I thank God I was in the position to do it.

Chapter 8

International Businessman

Terry speaking before an audience of hundreds.

So, to remind you, my background is in mechanical engineering and nuclear warfare.

Engineers aren't exactly known for our personalities. Normally, we're more associated with pocket protectors, glasses with tape on the middle, and snorting when we laugh. At farts. We think farts are hilarious. Or gross. It depends on if there are girls around. Not that we know anything about girls.

But let's just say we are not exactly known as the best salesmen.

Added to that, in the Air Force I basically practiced nuclear warfare. What I had to sell, no one wanted. Having the potential to end the world isn't on most people's Christmas list.

And now I was going to try to make a living selling stuff. In fact, in this case, selling skin cream.

Have you ever seen me? I'm not exactly the skin-cream kind of guy.

I am the "go out into the wilderness for days or weeks at a time without showering" kind of guy. But that doesn't sell well. Neither would the perfume that goes with it.

In my marketing business, it would be my job to recruit and train sales teams. I would get paid based on those teams' production. Believe it or not, Scouting prepared me for that as well. It taught me to inspire people. It taught me to be a leader.

See, I learned in Scouting that a true leader doesn't just lead people – he leads leaders. As a Senior Patrol Leader, you don't lead the troop; you lead the Patrol Leaders. You teach the Patrol Leaders how to better lead their patrols.

As a Scoutmaster, I don't lead the troop, I lead the Senior Patrol Leader. And I have 12 – count them – 12 Assistant Scoutmasters (God bless them!). They each advise a functional area of the troop. The biggest job I have is that of cheerleader.

I like to look at it like being the conductor of an orchestra. I don't play an instrument. My job is to lead – to inspire. I help those who play the instruments play the best they possibly can.

In Scouting, I learned to help people see the best in themselves; we do it all the time. I learned to inspire people to do better than they believe they can. I learned to see the good in people who may not even see it in themselves. Scouting taught me how.

This wasn't anything different.

If I could teach people who don't believe they can sell to sell, then I can build teams. If I can teach those team leaders to lead and inspire others, then I can build a company. If I can build that company to span the globe, then I can build an empire.

But it wasn't easy. For me, it was hard.

One of the worst times came very early in my business, while I was still in the Air Force.

With incredible effort, I had built up my income to where it finally was more than I was making as a Captain. This was extremely important for me, because I planned to get out of the Air Force, so I knew I'd better start making some real money.

And finally I did. My teams were growing. My income was growing. I could see the end in sight.

And then I lost a team of producers that made three-quarters of my income, literally overnight. They were all poached by a different company. Seventy-five percent of my income! Gone. No more. Just like that.

I was devastated. I had worked so hard to get there. There was finally some success, finally a light at the end of the tunnel, and that light ended up being the proverbial train that smashed into me head-on.

What could I do? I didn't have the strength to carry on. I couldn't get back up again and keep going. There was nothing left of me. No energy left in me to keep going.

But then again...

When I was completely exhausted on a 50-miler, with nothing left, I had found the strength.

When I was at Philmont Scout Ranch, hiking 50 miles in one day, I found the strength.

When trying to canoe against the wind on Lake Agnes at Charles L. Sommers wilderness canoe base, completely exhausted, I found the strength.

Maybe I could keep going. Maybe there was some strength in me still. Maybe I could get up one more time.

And one more time. And one more time.

Scouting taught me that I had more in me than I ever thought possible. That lesson, just like all the others, stayed with me as an adult.

Thank God. Because of that stamina I learned in Scouting, I ended up building back what I had lost, and a whole lot more. I've been extremely blessed in business, and have been able to retire early to raise my stepsons and see two of them become Eagle Scouts, as well as helping many, many other kids do the same.

What I do for fun in that retirement is a little different than most people, though…

Chapter 9

Adventures in the Wilderness

Terry on a sub-zero solo snowshoe backpacking excursion.

Some people like to golf. Others like to watch TV. I like to go into the wilderness, in some of the harshest environments on earth, and play around there.

I know: I'm kind of weird that way.

The great news is that Scouting gave me the skills to build on, so I can do so with confidence.

Before I tell about a couple of these experiences, I have to give a disclaimer: I go alone on many of them. I don't advise that at all. I've been trained by experts and practiced literally around the world, and I carry an emergency locator beacon everywhere I go that can alert that country's search and rescue forces to come and find me if the worst happens. So PLEASE, DO NOT go out by yourself. It's against the Guide to Safe Scouting, and it's unwise – as you're about to find out.

The Badlands

I was on a drive-about through South Dakota one scorching hot summer when I decided to go backpacking into Badlands National Park, 244,000 acres of harsh landscape with temperatures up to 116 degrees Fahrenheit. As I was bushwhacking through the scrub brush, I noticed that I was starting to make mistakes. I was starting to trip, and wasn't being as careful as I should be. I kept pushing forward and pushing forward, sweat pouring off of me, determined to push deep into the wilderness. I was using bad judgment.

If you're a Scout, you already see what was going on: heat exhaustion. If I had kept going, it would have gotten worse: heat stroke. That could have easily killed me. Thankfully, my Scout First Aid training kicked in, and I forced myself to do the right thing. I found a small tree and got under it. I loosened my clothing and took small sips of water. As I began to recover, I had a small snack to gain calories, and only then did I press on.

An excruciatingly hot day rewarded me with a sunset that burned red across the horizon, setting the opposing rock formations seemingly on fire as I sat beside a buffalo trail that had seen hundreds of years of history pass by.

And then it happened.

It started slowly at first. Just a flash here and there. I wasn't really sure I had seen something, in the distant blackening sky.

But an ominous darkness engulfed the previously blue and orange sky, lit up by eruptions of brightness, followed after a few seconds by a deep and rolling rumble.

Soon the explosions became fingers that reached from one horizon to the other, and the rumble became detonations coming from nowhere and everywhere all at once.

Being the tallest thing around for miles and miles in a lightning storm is a bit of an uneasy feeling, to say the least. But that feeling was equaled by the knowledge that going into the ravines around me could lead to drowning by the flash floods that can come from rain miles and miles away.

What would you do? Stay up top where the risk of lightning is greater, or go into a ravine with the potential of flash floods that come on as quickly as a fast-moving car? Either one could save your life, or end it.

Again, my Scout training kicked in. I analyzed the situation, considered my resources, and made my best decision based on the risks and rewards.

I chose to stay up top. I quickly rid myself of everything I could that was metal: my hiking poles, my backpack, everything I could think of. Then I positioned myself on top of my sleeping pad and bag, to give myself any insulation from the ground that I could in case lightning struck near me. I put out any vessel I could to try to catch some rain and build up my diminishing water supplies, and I prayed.

My prayers were answered: The storm abated before it hit me, but I was prepared. For life.

Sub-Zero Snowshoe Backpacking

If that trip was terribly hot, another one was just the opposite: extremely cold. The news reporters were telling everyone to stay inside as the winter temperatures went sub-zero in the eastern Washington area. That's like a siren's song to an adventurer.

My pack was especially heavy as I snowshoed up the mountain, leaving the safety of my 4-wheel drive behind when it could go no further. My hot breath froze the second it left my mouth, giving me the look of a locomotive steam engine as I chugged my way through the snow.

I screamed out as I thrust my heavy weight up higher and higher above the valley below. It didn't matter: There was no one around for miles, and even if there had been, the snow deadens any sound nearly as quickly as it comes out.

By the time I reached the top, I was completely exhausted. I threw my pack off and fell into the snow, unable to move. I was completely spent. I didn't have a single bit of energy left.

Until.

Until I saw the blizzard pummeling the mountain range on the other side of the valley, coming my way.

Suddenly I had all the energy in the world. I had no choice. Then again, I've been on hikes in Boy Scouts where I was completely exhausted, but kept going anyway. I had been on high adventures like Philmont and Sommers that pushed me to my limits. I knew I could go further than I thought I could, because Scouting taught me I could.

It was time to jump into action.

Depending on the situation, the first survival priority is shelter. And in this situation, if that storm hit before I was ready, none of the other priorities would matter.

Once again, my Scout training came to my aid. I needed a wind block for my tent, or my tent could be next to useless. It needed to be secured for the high winds that could be coming. There could be no gear left on the ground, or I would never find it again after the storm hit.

The storm advanced slowly, giving me time for my next priority: fire. Fire is easy when it's warm and dry out. It's harder when any firewood has been buried in several feet of snow for several weeks, or frozen solid and covered in frost if it's sticking above the snow.

Scouting taught me that inside every piece of wet wood is dry wood, so I went about gathering and processing anything I could. I dug down to the frozen solid ground and set my fire lay. Preferring to keep in practice, I pulled out my flint and steel and got to work. And work. And work... and work.

After quite some time of trying and failing, I tried the next step: matches. I know sound deadens in the snow, but I'm pretty sure I actually heard my matches laugh at me. In this cold dampness, there was no way in the world those were going to work. Okay, I hated to do it, but desperate times call for desperate measures, so I brought out the despised lighter.

Still no luck.

Wow.

Don't tell me I'm going to have to do the unthinkable! I make fun of people on a regular basis for this. I hate to admit this, especially in a book about Scouting, but it's the truth, so I have to say it, with my head hung low in shame:

I keep fire starters in my backpack in case of emergency, and suddenly it was becoming exactly that.

I worked at it, and worked at it. The storm, thank God, again played out before it hit me, so that was no longer a threat; but it was looking like it was going to be a long, cold night in the middle of nowhere on the top of a mountain in sub-zero temperatures without a fire.

Four long, arduous hours had passed since I had collapsed in the snow, exhausted, at the end of my climb, and I used the last ounce of any reserves I had in one last attempt on the fire. I fell over onto the snow beside my lifeless fire lay and prayed, as the frigid darkness encroached.

Isn't it funny how often we use as a last resort that one thing we really should do at the beginning? I believe prayers are always answered; but sometimes the answer is "no."

Not this time, though. As I lay there motionless, I saw a glimmer of light at the bottom of my fire lay.

Through my half-opened eyes, I saw that glimmer of light glow brighter. I sat up in disbelief and peered into the pit. Could it really be?

There was actually a flame! It was small, but it was there!

As I had done so many times on cold and rainy campouts as a Scout, I carefully fed the fire and gently blew on it until the small flicker became a bright, warm blaze.

I slept great that night on the frozen mountain, the last night I would sleep well for many months to come. The next morning I woke up to a gorgeous blue sky, surrounded by white trees and snow-covered mountain ranges for miles around. A lone wolf had passed by in the night, leaving nothing but his tracks in the snow.

I was amazed to find I had cell coverage on the top of that mountain, so checked my messages to find that my mom had suffered a stroke, fallen, hit her head, and broken her hip. The next 5 months were spent in ICU trying to save her life, only to be unsuccessful in the end.

But that trip into the wilderness gave me the strength I needed for the most challenging battle of my life.

And my next trip into the wilderness nearly ended mine.

The Arctic Circle

It's great having the confidence of Scout skills. If you've practiced them long enough, you can survive in some of the craziest places.

It was time for another adventure, so I was poring over my maps at my desk, looking for where that would be.

Hmmm, the Arctic Circle, I thought to myself. *It looks like there are roads of some kind all the way to somewhere called Inuvik in Northwest Territories of Canada. Then, even farther north, a place called Tuktoyaktuk, right on the Arctic Ocean. I don't see any roads. I wonder how you get there. I think I'll find out.*

A few days later, after doing some transmission work on my truck and getting some really good tires, I began my solo 6,000 mile driving, boating, and backpacking journey deep into the Arctic Circle.

When I arrived in Inuvik, I met an Inuvialuit guide by the name of Kylik who arranged to have me boated up into the Mackenzie Delta and dropped off on the permafrost to do some solo backpacking. After I'd returned exhausted, mosquito-bitten, and insanely happy from that little trip, he hit me with an honor I didn't expect:

"We need to get some meat to last through the winter, so we're going to hunt caribou. Would you like to go with us?" *Let me think,* I say to myself. *A group of Inuits in the Arctic Circle is asking me to go with them on a caribou hunt, something only they are allowed to do, and they rarely if ever ask a non-member. Uh, yeah; I'm gonna go with them on this.*

As a non-member, I wasn't allowed to hunt, though I carried a gun, as the grizzlies follow the herd and come running the minute they hear a shot. We hunted all night long, and came across the great herd at about 6 a.m. (Keep in mind that at this time of year, the sun never sets, so it's perfectly light all night long.)

To say it was amazing is like saying there's quite a bit of water in the ocean; it's an extreme understatement. Thousands of caribou spread across the permafrost for as far as you could see. This was the great herd I had read about, and I was actually out hunting them with a group of Inuits deep in the Arctic Circle. It's amazing the adventures that Scouting prepares you for!

They shot six of them, enough to last awhile, and we spent the next 6 hours processing and hauling the meat. As we were doing it, the winds kept getting stronger and stronger. The temperatures, though already cold, were dropping drastically. By the time we got the last of the meat loaded into their truck, we were in a full-blown Arctic storm.

Have you ever gotten a feeling in the pit of your stomach that doesn't make sense, but you felt was true anyway?

For some unknown reason, I felt like I needed to head south.

Now.

Kylik and his friends were amazed. "You're crazy!" they said. "It's too dangerous with this storm. You have to come back north to Inuvik with us."

One of them even invited me to his family's whaling village, an honor rarely offered to anyone outside of their family, let alone some non-native that they just met a few days ago!

Add to that that I was exhausted from hunting and carrying meat all night, and covered in blood from head to toe.

Then came the final nail in the coffin: I was out of gas. There weren't exactly any gas stations around, and I had already used all the gas in my Jerry cans. It was okay, though; the driver of the other truck had a Jerry can that Kylik said I could split with them. The problem was, he didn't tell the other driver that, and he had already emptied it into his truck.

So now I'm almost out of gas, exhausted, covered in blood, deep in the Arctic Circle in an arctic storm.

"You have to come back with us now," they pleaded. "It's impossible to make it down to the town with a gas station. There's no way you can make it."

But that feeling in the pit of my stomach kept telling me that I had to try. So we hugged our goodbyes, and I headed south in uncertainty.

No matter how bumpy the road was, I had a hard time staying awake. I would pull over for minutes at a time, but didn't dare stay long. When I got to the top of a hill, I would coast down the other side to save gas. When I reached the ferry to cross the river, I'm sure I looked like an axe murderer, covered in blood like I was. I prayed constantly, though I knew I didn't have a prayer. Again, prayers are always answered, though sometimes the answer is "no."

But again, not this time. That intense wind I had was a tail wind, and it gave me just enough gas to coast into the gas station on fumes.

I pitched my tent right by a trickling stream near Dawson City, Yukon, where the gold rush started, and decided to put my coat, pants, and gun belt in the stream to soak off some of the blood. As an afterthought, I placed a big rock on each of them. Thank God I did.

When I woke up some hours later, the stream was no longer there. It had been replaced by a raging river, right by my tent. "My gear!" I exclaimed. "My only coat! My pants! My gun belt! There's no way they can still be down there under this current!" But I had to check.

Wading into a river swollen by an arctic storm is no fun, but feeling for your gear under the water with your feet and realizing you have to get even more wet to get them out is even less fun.

Later that day I saw a man and asked him, "Do you have any idea why the creek is so swollen?"

"Sure!" he said. "There's a huge arctic storm going on up north!"

"Yeah, I knew that," I told him. "I just came from up there."

"Wait a minute. You just came down the Dempster?"

"Yep, it's the only road. I came down just a few hours ago. Why?"

"You're kidding," he said in astonishment. "A large segment of the Dempster doesn't exist anymore! It washed out. You can't come down it anymore. That ferry you came across on is somewhere downstream now. I doubt they'll ever find it!"

If I hadn't listened to that feeling in the pit of my stomach, I would have either been trapped up north, or washed out along with the road or ferry.

If your heart tells you "yes" but your brain tells you "no," follow your heart. It will take you places your mind couldn't conceive of.

That's just a couple of examples of the adventures I've been able to go on because of Scouting. If you're interested, I have some pictures and a few more stories on my website at www.TerryLFossum.com.

Where did I get the foundation of skills I built on to go on these adventures?

Campouts. Never miss a campout. Especially the challenging ones that include rain, really hot or cold weather, or hiking. These are the ones that challenge you. These are the ones that make you tough.

In fact, have patrol campouts! Those are the most fun of all of them, because your patrol can do whatever it wants, whenever it wants!

And please listen closely: I was tempted to back out of Scouting, like everyone else, when I reached 16 years old. I had a girlfriend, I could drive, I was extremely involved in all sorts of activities in and outside of school; but I'm really glad I stuck with it. That's the age where you're really starting to hone your adventure skills. You've got the basic skills down; now it's time to perfect your advanced skills.

If I hadn't kept going in Scouting until I was 18 (and even after with the Order of the Arrow), there's no way I would have attained the skills needed to go on these adventures, or to win a survival reality show against some of the best survivalists in the nation!

Chapter 10

Survival Show

Terry in survival shelter.

Are you kidding me?

A television reality show?

I don't even watch much TV! And I really don't watch much *reality* TV!

Sure, I've seen some *Survivor* and *Fear Factor* and such, and that's why I swore I'd never be on one! Have you seen the crap they make them eat? Why would I want to do something like that?

But here I was, my youngest boys (twins) just turning 18 and getting their Eagle (do I hear an "Amen"?!), so I'm ready to come out of retirement, and had been praying to God: "Okay, God, what do you want me to do next?" Then someone who had gone through a Wood Badge course I staffed answered a casting call on my behalf and says to them, "You really ought to talk to Terry; he'd be great!"

So I get this email out of the blue saying, "We're from a new survival reality TV show, and we'd like to talk to you!"

I didn't want to be on a reality TV show! It's been a few years since my last adventure, and I'm old! And fat! And very comfortable right where I am, thank you.

Here's the problem: If you've been praying to God to show you the way and He shows you, you can't say, "No, that's not what I was thinking! Can you show me something easier?"

Now, let me be honest with you: I didn't think there was a prayer in the world that I could win this thing. My belief was that I was there for a Reason, but I doubted that Reason was for me to win it. It had to be something else.

So I called this entire thing "blind faith." I would do the show with the full understanding that I wasn't there for myself. I was there for whatever reason God had for me, and with the faith that He would guide me if I would shut up and listen to Him. That reason might be to help someone else win, and I had to be good with that.

A Scout is always reverent – not just when it suits him.

The first person I met from the cast was Ben. Ben was a strong young man in his twenties, an Air Force SERE Instructor. That stands for Survival, Evasion, Resistance, and Escape. This guy spends his entire adult life teaching people how to survive in the worst climates around the world while evading enemy troops behind enemy lines! Then he teaches them what to do if they're caught: how to resist torture, keep from giving away our nation's secrets, and escape from whatever prison they put them in. This guy LIVES survival!

The second person I met was Brady. Are you kidding me??? Brady was a Marine Scout Sniper! He's spent time surviving on his own in some of the worst war zones in the world, hunting out the enemy and, well, sniping them! This is one of the toughest people I've ever met!

And I kept meeting more and more of them. A battle-hardened former Marine, another SERE instructor, a man who teaches armies around the world how to best kill people. THIS IS WHAT I'M UP AGAINST?!

I can see why they threw in their token Boy Scout from the Fossil Patrol: to give everyone someone to laugh at.

Little did they know…

They didn't realize how tough Boy Scouts really are! They didn't realize how well prepared we are to meet any challenge.

They didn't realize that we spend all sorts of time in patrols and troops, learning how to work with other kids and adults. And how we've already been tested at camporees and on high adventures, on campouts in the rain and cold, and on hikes where very few people go. Boy Scouts are some of the toughest kids around – and they turn into tough adults.

Okay, so you've heard all about how Scouting helped me in business, in the military, in public speaking, and all of that. But how in the world did it help me win a reality TV show?

Here's how.

Scout Skills

I always wondered: Aside from winning a blue ribbon, why do I have to know this stuff? When am I ever going to need to know how to tie a knot or start a fire in the rain? Little did I know that someday it would help me win a quarter of a million dollars. As you've read, these skills also kept me alive several times when a non-Scout might have died.

Every single Scout skill was critical in the jungle: knots and lashings, first aid, fire building, navigation, knife safety, backpacking, cooking (what little food there was), and more.

Even things you wouldn't think of: skills like watching the clouds and listening to the birds so you knew when rain was on the way, or observing your surroundings while you're hiking so that you notice resources for eating or building your shelter were critical.

One of the Scout skills I didn't expect to ever come in handy was that of eating nasty food – and trying not to throw up. But there I was, eating a live grub the size of a cigar and licking up the guts that had squirted out of my mouth onto the table! How did Scouting prepare me for that?

Boy Scout cooking! In our troop, the patrols compete for the Golden Spoon Award at each campout, given to the patrol that cooks the best meal while working well together, and cleaning their dishes correctly. As Scoutmaster, I would have the dubious opportunity of being one of the judges, along with my SPL, so I had to sample every meal.

OH. MY. GOSH.

Newer Scouts, even those who used to complain about their parents' cooking, find ways of massacring food that I could never imagine.

And the best part of it? They're proud of it!

There are three ranges of doneness: raw, burned, or both. How they could figure out how to burn part of a meal while having the other part still actually cold, I have no idea. Pancakes are a great example of this. I have actually eaten pancakes that were completely black on the outside, but still runny on the inside. How do you accomplish this?

But my job, no matter how raw, burned, or completely unrecognizable the dish was, would be to put it in my mouth and find something good to say about it as these Scouts, as proud as they could be, presented me with what might be my last meal ever.

So how did this "skill" help me out on the show? Picture that cigar-sized live grub squirting out of your mouth as you bite into it, and you licking the excess guts off the table in front of you.

Yep. Not too much unlike those pancakes!

I've used all the Scouting skills many, many times in my life. From staying cool in the deserts of Egypt, to navigating the mountains of Rwanda looking for the elusive silverback gorillas, to surviving in the jungles of the Rupununi. I've thanked God, and Scouting, for them many, many times.

Camporees

I didn't realize it at the time, but camporees helped prepare me for competing in the business world, in the military, and big time in preparing me for the show. If you haven't been to a camporee, this is where troops compete against each other in Scout skills like knot tying, fire building, and first aid.

These camporee events were *exactly* like the competitions we had during the show! Think about it: What the show called "survival skills," we call "Scouting skills!" It's the kind of stuff we do all the time: fire building, knot tying, obstacle courses, slingshots, canoeing. Yep, sounds like Scouting skills to me. And the most important part was being able to apply these skills under the pressure of competition.

I didn't always do great at the competitions, but I didn't always do great at camporees, either. But making the effort taught me how to lose, which is much more important than learning how to win. Being a good winner is easy. Losing and getting back up, dusting yourself off, and trying harder next time – that's a skill that helps you keep going when the times get tough.

Summer Camp

I told you how much I loved summer camp. Do you know what my favorite merit badge at summer camp was? Wilderness Survival! Go figure!

How cool is the Wilderness Survival merit badge? You get to go out in the middle of nowhere, build a shelter, and sleep in it overnight! My instructor taught me how to build a solar still so I could get water in the middle of a desert. I learned what plants I could eat and how to trap animals. This kind of knowledge made me part of an extremely small group of people in the country that could actually survive if we had to. Hey, if there's a zombie apocalypse, I'm your man! And so is everyone else who earned the Wilderness Survival merit badge.

I found out on the show that I was actually very well prepared for surviving in the wilderness; I could keep up with the other survivalists, and then some! Now, I'm not saying I knew everything, and I certainly learned a lot from every one of them; but I was much better prepared than even I thought I would be. Years and years of starting fires without matches and sleeping outdoors in some really rough conditions didn't hurt, either.

I also mentioned earlier that I was on summer camp staff. Do you know what the best part was? I got to TEACH Wilderness Survival!!! It was awesome! I got to take groups of kids out to the wilderness and teach them all of this cool stuff. Because we always learn more from teaching, I got better and better at it year after year.

I loved it when my students were making their shelters without being able to use tarps, ropes, or anything else. During the day, they kept coming up to me and asking, "Is my shelter good enough? Is my shelter good enough?" Finally, after about the millionth time I'd heard that, I started telling them, "Okay, here's the deal: I always wake up in the middle of the night, because I have to pee. It's pretty dark out, so there's pretty good odds that I'm going to pee on your shelter. So, let me ask you: Is your shelter good enough?"

My students had the best shelters you've ever seen.

And I learned how to teach people to survive in the wilderness – something that came in very handy when helping my novice partner.

High Adventure

So why was it that an old guy in his 50s was able to compete against these younger men and women in their 20s and 30s? Because I've done high adventure! I've been on several 50-milers, both on foot and in canoes.

As Scouts, we learn to push ourselves to our limits, and then go further. We learn that we have more strength inside of us than we think we have. We've been exhausted, and cold, and wet, and hungry. And we've learned to love it!

Charles L. Sommers Canoe Base is in Ely, Minnesota, just south of the Canadian border. I grew up in the extreme southern tip of Texas, over 1,700 miles from there, and when I was about 14 years old a group of us Scouts took an old, beat-up school bus all the way there – more than 26 hours of driving spread over several days. We camped along the way, played cards, screamed, yelled, and had a general good time. The canoeing itself was epic. We could drink right out of the lake – no boiling the water or filtering. We caught fish to go with the food we brought. We would swamp our canoes and go swimming – all the things kids like to do. It all changed when we got back to base camp, though.

We found out there was a hurricane heading directly for our town. Our homes, our families, and everything else were right in the way. It was going to hit in 48 hours. We couldn't drive at the same pace we had on the way up. We would get there after the hurricane arrived. You can't drive into a hurricane – chances are, you'll die.

Our two choices were either to wait it out and come into town after it was all over, hoping for the best for our families, or to drive the 26-plus hours straight, and try to beat it. The choice was clear. Scouting had taught us all responsibility – responsibility to our families and our communities. If there was a battle to be fought, we wanted to help fight it. We were Boy Scouts, after all. Scouting has a long history of helping out in intense situations.

That was also the first time I was part of a life-or-death decision. When we drove into town, the rains were already hitting, and hitting hard. But we made it, and we were there for those we loved.

Philmont Scout Ranch was the second place I was part of a life-or-death situation, and the decision was completely in my hands. If you haven't heard about Philmont, it's more than 140,000 acres of adventure in the Sangre de Cristo Mountains of New Mexico. You can take any trek from easy to hard, or you can go completely crazy and go "Rayado." Rayado is a 21-day experience known as The Ultimate Wilderness Challenge. You hike your butts off in these beautiful mountains, practice wilderness first aid, backcountry emergency procedures, group dynamics, navigation, with all sorts of little "surprises" thrown in, while evading bears and lightning storms.

Why do you think I was able to compete well on the show?

I was 16 when I did this! We hiked over 50 miles in ONE DAY with full packs in the mountains! We practiced every single skill I needed to have on the show, for 21 days straight. Add in all the competing I did at camporees, and there wasn't much new they could throw at me!

It's funny: All the time we were doing this, I didn't realize how much I was learning. I didn't realize it was setting me up for success in life. All I knew is that I was having fun. I was going on adventures, and adventure is cool.

These days we go on adventures on video games. I know: They're fun. I play them, too. But they're not real adventures. You're not actually going anywhere. You're sitting in your chair. You're not really in any danger. If you die, you respawn.

That's not the way it was on the mountain that day at Philmont.

We were climbing to the top of some mountain. I don't remember the name; we went over a lot of them. But as we were nearing the top, a thunderstorm started coming our way. Now, thunder means lightning, and lightning can mean death. Especially when you're near the top of a mountain, the tallest thing around, with a metal-framed backpack on your back.

Here's the crazy part: The entire group looked at me and asked, "What do we do?"

See, somewhere near the beginning of the trip, we had decided to pick a leader, and that leader ended up being me. That's all fine and good, but suddenly there I was, 16 years old, and expected to make a decision that might be life-or-death for eight of my fellow Scouts.

And they wonder why Scouts become so responsible. We're put in leadership situations and expected to make decisions! The adults don't get in the way; they let us make the decisions and then live with them. Or not live with them, as the case may be.

Here were my choices: Keep going forward over the mountain and hope for the best. Our destination was on the other side of the mountain, and we had a lot of miles to cover still. Or, backtrack down the mountain and lose all that time and elevation we had worked hard to gain. Who knew how long the storm would last, and at some point it was going to get dark.

The storm was getting closer and closer. The sky was getting very dark. The thunder was booming. And everyone was looking at me.

"Okay, here's what we're going to do," I finally said. "A few minutes or hours aren't worth losing our lives over. We're going to backtrack down the mountain and spread out, so if one of us gets hit, we won't all get hit. The rest of us can perform first aid and go get help. Then, we're going to put our packs down with the metal off the ground, and sit on them so we're not touching the ground, in case the lightning strikes nearby and travels through the ground. Put your raingear on, and pray. Let's do this!"

We scrambled back down the mountain and spread out like we'd planned. After several minutes, the storm passed and we continued our hike safe and sound, living to hike another day.

Just a few years later I was an officer in the United States Air Force, making command decisions where a lot was at stake. I thought back to this day often. Scouting prepared me to handle the stress and perform under pressure – even when real lives were at stake.

National Youth Leadership Training and Wood Badge

National Youth Leadership Training (NYLT) is a week-long leadership training course for Scouts. It's awesome. In fact, it's probably some of the most fun, and definitely the best leadership training, you could possibly have as a youth. Wood Badge is the adult equivalent, and it too is amazing. Both don't just help you learn more about Scouting; they help you learn about working better with people outside of Scouting as well, among many other things.

And in this case, I thanked God I had been to both of them.

Everyone who watched the show saw my partner and me get into a *serious* argument. It doesn't matter why; the bottom line is, we were both exhausted and stressed out, coming from completely different backgrounds, thrown into an intense situation while trying to compete.

Wait a minute – that kind of sounds like a patrol, doesn't it? Or a corporate team. Or a military unit.

Some of the best corporate and military trainings in the world teach this, but the problem is, too many people in the world never get to go to those trainings.

Scouts do.

I learned that the four stages of team development are Forming, Storming, Norming, and Performing. I learned that you can't get to the Performing stage of growth without going through the others, and that includes Storming.

Time out – does that mean that if your team is going to perform, you have to have some fights?

Yes, that's exactly right.

You have to address and work through the issues in a respectful manner, or the team can never operate at its fullest potential.

So that also means that if your team (your patrol, committee, or whatever it is) is fighting, that's not necessarily a bad thing. It can actually be an extremely good thing, depending on how you handle it!

And the Managing Conflict class teaches you how to handle it.

My Scouting training allowed me to share those stages of team development, and gave me the realization that what we were going through was natural, and even good; that we needed to work through our differences to become strong. Iron only becomes steel when it goes through the fire.

And as you saw on the show, things changed immediately for us. We began to work together instead of pulling apart. Instead of pointing out each other's failings, we pointed out each other's successes. We didn't place blame – we accepted responsibility. It was no longer about "me," and became about "us."

We became a team – a team that won the show.

If you haven't gone to NYLT or Wood Badge yet, you need to go. It's a blast. If you have gone, do everything you can to be on staff. It's even more of a blast. As a Scout, I went to a course called Brownsea II. Then it changed to TLT, and TLD, and several other names over the years. And I think I've been to all of them, as a participant, or a staff member, or Course Director. I've been on Wood Badge staff for many years, and I keep on learning every single time I do it.

Leadership

The most important factor in winning the show wasn't so much the survival skills, but rather leadership. Think about it: My job on the show was to take a person who was not used to being in the outdoors and help them through it.

That's what we do in Scouts all the time, isn't it? We take new Scouts who are scared to death, inexperienced, and unsure of themselves, and help them along! We find reasons to praise them to build their confidence, and slowly give them bigger challenges to conquer, while guiding them and reassuring them every step of the way!

The second most important thing we learn in Scouting, in my opinion, is leadership. Any chance I get to learn from others is time well spent! It helps in your personal life, your professional life, *all* of your life!

In Scouts, I jumped at every leadership position I could, including Senior Patrol Leader, Junior Assistant Scoutmaster, and even Order of the Arrow Section Vice-Chief for much of Texas. Like I mentioned, I was on camp staff, Junior Leadership Training Staff (now NYLT) – everything I could, I did.

As an adult, I've held nearly every position on the unit, district, and council levels as well. Every step of the way, I'm learning more and more that I'm able to use in other aspects of my life.

Ethics

So if leadership is the second most important thing we learn in Scouting, what would the most important thing be?

No question: Ethics.

A leader needs to have ethics. A leader needs to have a good moral compass, and there is no better moral compass than the Scout Law.

We all recite the Scout Law every week, and most of us know it so well we don't even think about it when we say the words!

Why do we even have a Scout Law, except that it sounds really cool?

Let's face it: None of us really go by the Scout Law 100% of the time. I don't. I'm not perfect. And odds are that you don't, either. And, believe it or not, that's okay.

I've heard that the most important word in the Scout Law is "is," because a Scout IS all of those things. I don't agree. That's a false expectation. It's impossible.

So if nobody actually does it 100% of the time, why even have it? Because it acts as a guide. It's something we try our best to do.

Do you know what my biggest fear of going on this show was? I knew that I was going to be representing Boy Scouts. I was going to be wearing the uniform throughout the whole show, and that I was going to be on camera 24 hours a day, 7 days a week, for an entire month, if I lasted that long!

Now, listen, guys: I'm not that perfect! I mean, I try real hard, but I'm going to slip up! I do my best to live the Scout Oath and Law every single day of my life, but guess what? I'm human! So, let me ask you this: How would YOU do? Could you be perfect?

Let's add to that: You haven't eaten a single meal in a long, long time. You are literally starving. You haven't had a night's sleep for equally as long. You've frozen at night, and sweated your butt off during the day. You're completely sleep deprived. You haven't showered forever, and you smell like the south end of a northbound dog. And, by the way, every person you're around (except your partner) is your competition for a quarter of a million dollars. Could you be perfect?

Okay, I think we're on the same page.

But, just as with everything else, I decided I'd do my best (where have we heard that phrase before?), just like I try to do every single day. If I slipped up, then I'd just hope people would understand.

So if you slip up, don't beat yourself up for it. Learn from it, and remember the lesson the next time you're in that situation.

Trustworthy

On the show, I was competing for ¼ million dollars. We've all seen how people lie to each other on shows like this, and talk behind people's backs.

Scouts don't act that way. We show people a different way of life, a way where people have honor; where the very first point of their Law is "trustworthy."

Why do we do that?

Well, first of all, for the most important reason of all: because it's the right thing to do.

Add to that that people will like you only if they know they can trust you. If you lie, they lose respect for you. If they lose respect for you, they won't want to be around you, and they certainly won't follow you as a leader. If they know they can't trust you, there's no way for them to know if you have their best interests at heart, or are just using them to get what you want. Think about it: Who do you know who's a liar? Would you want to be their friend? Would you want them to be the Senior Patrol Leader of your troop?

That's why it's important to tell the truth, even if it will get you into trouble. Guard your integrity. As a leader, you have to be trustworthy. If your people can't trust you, they won't follow you. If they know you tell the truth and have their best interests in mind, they'll follow you to the ends of the earth!

Loyal

It seems like loyalty is a rare commodity these days.

BFFs change like Scouts change their underwear at camp: about once a week!

There's a phrase in business: "If you want loyalty, get a dog." All too often, companies aren't loyal to their employees. Back several years ago, you could plan on working for the same company for 30 years, and getting a retirement for your golden years.

In many cases, things have changed drastically. As soon as times get tough, the layoffs start, and employees who have been loyal, hard workers throughout the years find themselves on the streets.

It's not just companies that exhibit this behavior, though. All too often, employees are job searching on company time, sometimes even on company computers, looking for a better offer to jump at.

Often people talk behind others' backs, and look for ways to pull themselves up by pulling others down.

Scouts are taught differently. We're taught to take care of each other. Whether it's at a troop meeting or on a 50-mile hike, you take care of your buddy.

We're even taught something called the Buddy System: You don't go swimming or in the outdoors without your buddy. Your life may depend on it! We take that lesson into all aspects of our lives. People know they can count on a Scout.

I think it's time to change that saying to: "If you want loyalty, get a Scout."

Loyalty builds strong teams. It builds strong patrols, strong troops, strong companies, strong families. When people know you've got their back, they're more likely to work for the common good, instead of just themselves. Loyalty is yet another great quality Scouts bring to the world.

If you want loyalty, get a Scout!

Helpful

A few years ago my family and I were on vacation, driving through Idaho, pulling a pop-up camper. Suddenly, at 60 m.p.h., a wheel flew off of the camper! Sparks flew as the metal ground into the pavement, damaging what was left of the hub beyond repair. We were in trouble. We had three young children in the middle of nowhere with a camper that couldn't be moved. And it was getting dark fast.

What we didn't notice was the truck pulling a flatbed trailer passing us as we sat by the road. Driving that truck were Kirk Widmer and his adult son, Kevin Widmer. Kirk was a Scout volunteer, and Kevin is an Eagle Scout.

Being true Scouts, they turned around to see if we needed help, thank God. They stayed and helped until 1:00 in the morning, loading our camper up on their trailer, driving us to the nearest town that had a repair service, and making sure we were okay for the night.

And like true Scouts, they absolutely refused any money in return. Kirk and Kevin won't say that they were knights in shining armor. They will only say that they were Scouts.

A Scout is helpful, even when he may not want to be. Heck, anyone can be helpful when they want to be; that's no big deal. Scouts are a big deal. They go above and beyond. They do things not because it's convenient, but for the most important reason of all: It's the right thing to do.

There are countless examples of how Scouts exhibit the points of the Scout Oath and Law every day across the country, and even around the world.

And the Oath and Law are really the most important things we learn in Scouting, aren't they?

It's not just about the Scout skills, though it is about them. It's not just about teamwork, though it is about it. It's not just about the great outdoors, and adventures, and funny songs and stupid skits, though it is about those things too.

But it's about something much more important.

It's about a way of life.

It's about not just being *in* Scouts, but *being* a Scout.

It's about being a better citizen. It's about making the world a better place.

It's about doing something not just because it helps you. It's about doing it because it's the right thing to do.

It's about being Honorable Men and Women.

Wait a minute. Can that really work? Isn't this supposed to be a competitive world? Don't you have to be the best to win? No, you have to be *your* best to win. I've been very successful in the military, in business, and other aspects of my life by following the part of the Scout Oath that says, "Help other people at all times."

There's a reason the fleur-de-lis on the Scout badge was usually on the north point of a compass. The Scout Oath and Law will always lead you in the right direction.

In the winning scene for the entire show, I carried the torch for my partner, Natalie, and handed it to her so she could light the cauldron that signaled the win.

I learned that, too, from Scouting. That's the same thing the Scoutmaster does for the Senior Patrol Leader. He sets him up for success, and then lets him lead the way. In a youth-led troop, the Scoutmaster doesn't have the spotlight – the Senior Patrol Leader does. And a smart Senior Patrol Leader does the same thing for his Patrol Leaders, who do the same thing for their patrol members. Behind them all are the Troop Committee members who work tirelessly behind the scenes, and the Professional Scouters who do everything in their power to create an environment for success.

True leadership is helping others see the vision, and helping them achieve it while feeling great about doing so.

Conclusion

Terry receives Eagle Scout from Scoutmaster Jerry White.

So I'd love to take credit for all of this and say how cool I am, but I am only what Scouting taught me to be. It was my first Patrol Leader, Donald Davis, who taught me how to make people feel good about themselves. It was my SPL, my brother Greg, who showed me how to inspire people to WANT to take action. It was my OA Lodge Chief, John Vanderput, who showed me compassion. My Lodge Advisor, Steve Vasberg, showed me organization; my brother Mike and all the members of my summer camp staff showed me how to lead while having fun.

It's all the adults, and the kids, whom I worked with then and whom I work with today, that continue to inspire me every single day. It's my sons, who remind me about the difference we're making in kids' lives.

So, if you're a Scout, stick with it. No matter what, stick with it. *No matter what.* I don't care what your excuse is for thinking about quitting – don't do it. And earn your Eagle. I can't tell you how many people I've talked to who were in Scouts but didn't make Eagle, and they regret it for the rest of their lives. They tell me why they quit, why it made so much sense to them at the time, and why it ended up being the dumbest thing they ever did.

You may wonder if Scouting is making a difference in your life, but it is, I promise you. Just by being around it, you're learning to be a better person. In fact, I'd go so far as to say that you're learning to be one of the best people in the world. Seriously. I've been around the world. I've met a lot of people. None of them are better than Scouts. Hey, that's what Scouts teaches us. On every step of our trail to Eagle.

Remember: It's your life. It's your future. You're in charge of it; no one else is. It's no one else's job to get you to Eagle. It's no one else's responsibility. Don't be like so many others I talked to who thought they were getting back at someone else by quitting. I almost quit, and it would have affected the rest of my life, and not in a good way.

If I had quit, you wouldn't be reading this book right now. You might have been reading about me in the newspaper – but maybe not for a good reason.

You know where I come from. You know that I wasn't expected to grow up to be anything. But Scouting changed all of that.

In fact, I want to congratulate you for making it this far. Hey, Scouting is fun, but it's not easy! It takes a tough person to go on those campouts even when the weather's bad. It takes a tough person to go on 50-milers, carrying everything you need on your back or in your canoe.

Do you think summer camp isn't tough? Guess what: Sleeping in a tent for a week is tougher than what most of the people in this country can handle. I know. I've met them.

That's right: Even if we're having fun doing it, it's toughening us up, and teaching us lessons that will make us the leaders of the world tomorrow.

Will you end up being a business leader, a community leader, or a military leader, or, the most important thing of all, an Honorable Man or Woman? That's completely up to you, but I can tell you this: You're learning everything you need right where you're at: in Scouts.

If you're an Eagle Scout: Scouting has given you wings. Now you must fly.

If you're an adult reading this, first of all, THANK YOU. You're the exact type of person who had a dramatic impact on my life. You will never know all of the lives you've changed because you encouraged some kid like me when he needed it most. Or you believed in him when he didn't believe in himself.

You're showing the example of what it's like to grow up to be a good person, just by being a good person yourself. Those kids are watching you – I guarantee it. They're watching every move you make. And they're emulating you.

The difference you're making in the world will last long after you're gone. The kids you're teaching today will teach others, who will teach others, who will teach still others, for generations.

I think all of us want to feel we're making a difference, that the world will be a better place because we were in it. Scouting gives us that place to actually do it. To make that difference. To change those lives.

But check this out: I'm going to ask you to do even more.

Volunteer at the district and council levels. It's actually really fun. I didn't think I was cool enough, or rich enough, or important enough, but as it turns out, those people are Scouters just like us who care about kids.

Many of them have been doing the job for too long, though, and need help.

If you've ever thought, *I wish the camporees were more fun*, or *I wish Scouting For Food was run better*, or *The popcorn sales weren't run well*, or *STEM University should've been better organized*, or whatever, jump in! It doesn't matter what your background is, or your level of expertise, or even how much time you have – your enthusiasm is needed.

Even if you don't have kids in the program anymore, please continue to help out. I did, and still do, even though my kids "aged out." You believe in the program. You believe in what it does for youth. It's not just your kids who need you. Others do, too – other kids who aren't lucky enough to have parents like you.

And I know it's not cool to talk about money, but we need to.

Scouting needs your donations, whatever they may be.

Look, we need the best people possible at the Scout Office. And I can tell you that other nonprofits and corporations are circling around like buzzards to try to steal our professional Scouters. Hey, these people are some of the best trained there are in dealing with people, recruiting, running organizations, and so on.

Sure, they do it because they care about the youth and about the cause, but they have families to raise, and mouths to feed just like you and me. And almost every single one of them is getting paid less than they could be somewhere else.

Our camps need funding or they quickly fall into ruin, and then kids won't want to go to them. Video games are more cool than a beat-up, neglected camp. If you can't donate money, donate time to help maintain your camp. It's actually a lot of fun to get out there with a couple of your friends and build or paint or something.

All right, I've said my piece.

Since so many Scouting events end with a Scoutmaster Minute(s), I'd like to end with one here.

As my own personal last Scoutmaster Minute ever (I'm passing the job on very soon), I'd like to end with one of my favorite stories about Lord Baden-Powell, the founder of Scouting. I don't know if the story is true or not, but there's a lesson in it, either way.

Lord Baden-Powell (BP) was an avid outdoorsman who loved sleeping outside throughout his military and Scouting careers. It's rumored that he preferred to sleep outside even when he was home!

But BP was getting old, and he just couldn't do it anymore.

He decided he wanted to spend one more night camping out, and of course wanted to do it with a Scout.

But he wanted this Scout to be special, so he went around during a camporee and spoke to several Scouts to decide whom he would take on his final camping trip ever.

He went up to one Scout and asked, "What do you do best, young man?"

"Me, Lord Baden-Powell? I'm a wonderful cook. I can make things in a Dutch oven that could be served in a five-star restaurant."

BP smiled and went on to the next boy.

"Scout, what do you do best?"

"I'm the fastest at tying knots that you'll ever meet. You can barely see my hands, they're flying so fast!"

The Scout showed BP, and he was indeed duly impressed.

He went on asking other Scouts the same question, and the answers varied with each Scout.

"I'm great at first aid!"

As old as I am, that might come in handy! BP chuckled to himself.

"I can take a canoe down Class 4 rapids and come out dry as a bone!"

"I'm the best at repelling you've ever seen!" (BP knew the Scout meant "rappelling," but he didn't correct him. He just thought it was funny.)

But one boy's answer perplexed him.

"BP, I can sleep at night."

Lord Baden-Powell didn't know what he meant, so he went on talking to more and more boys who gave more and more answers.

But his thoughts kept going back to the one. "I can sleep at night."

Well, I've never heard that one before, he thought. *So, let's give that a try.*

So they went on BP's last-ever camping trip, and it was quite uneventful.

I mean, it was nice and all, but nothing out of the ordinary for a Scout.

That night, rain woke BP from a sound sleep. He could hear from the snoring in the tent next to him that it wasn't bothering the boy at all.

Yep, he can sure sleep at night! BP thought. *I guess I'll have to take care of camp.*

So he got up to cover up the firewood, and found it was already done. And he went to put away the camp chairs, and they were already under the tarp with the firewood. Since they were the old-style canvas tents, he knew he'd better loosen the ropes, or the canvas could shrink and tear. But it had been done already.

Everything that needed to be done already was. And the Scout who had done those things was sleeping soundly.

That's what he means, BP thought. *No wonder he can sleep at night.*

Scouting prepares us for life.

Not just any life, but a life well-lived. A life of making a difference. A life of honor. A life that lets us sleep very, very well at night.

So that's my story. And I know it's just one of millions, but it's the one I know best, because it's my story.

What's your Scouting story?

You're living it right now.

Scouting is teaching you all of these great outdoor skills that you'll use for the rest of your life. It's teaching you the leadership that people will look to when times get tough. It's teaching you the ethics that we need so much more of in this world today.

Will Baden-Powell's dream of Scouting changing the world come true? I can't say for sure, but I can say that from the Scouts I've met, it looks like it really is.

We're making a difference. We're changing the world.

The future is in your hands, and they're good hands. Because they're the hands of a Scout.

So, from one Scout to another:

Live with adventure. Live with honor. Live like a Scout.

Your friend,

Terry